I0071532

ACCOUNTING 101

FOR THE

START-UP ENTREPRENEUR

ACCOUNTING 101

FOR THE

START-UP ENTREPRENEUR

What I need to know about handling
money when I start my own company

Margery Phelps

Cherokee ✦ Rose
Publishing, LLC
INFORM, INSPIRE, ENTERTAIN

Copyright © 2020 by Margery Phelps.

All rights reserved. The text and illustrations of this publication, or any part thereof, may not be reproduced or transmitted in any electrical, mechanical or printed form or by any means, without prior written permission of the copyright owner.

This book is for general information only and is not intended to make financial decisions or provide financial advice, or replace opinions of CPAs or Financial Planners. The publisher and author assume no responsibility for errors or omissions nor any liability for damages resulting from the use of information provided herein.

This publication contains opinions and ideas of the author and is sold with the understanding that the publisher and author are not engaged in rendering professional accounting and/or financial services and/or advice. Should the reader require advice or personal assistance with the subject matter of this publication, they are encouraged to seek the advice of a competent and licensed professional.

WEBSITES:

www.MargeryPhelps.com

www.CherokeeRosePublishing.com

www.SBAfundingdepot.com

ISBN: 978-0-9994622-1-8

Cherokee ❖ Rose
Publishing, LLC
INFORM, INSPIRE, ENTERTAIN

TABLE OF CONTENTS

FOREWORD

Having practiced law for more than 40 years and with a B.B.A from Emory University in accounting, I have a fundamental grasp of business that has been applied throughout my career.

I learned a significant amount from Margery's book. She states the text in the context of entertaining simplicity.

Margery and I found each other through an ad for a bookkeeping assistant. Little did I know she would become a confidant, an organizational expert , friend and so much more.

This book will be required reading for my children, grandchildren and friends and I will encourage them to keep it close for reference purposes.

Wayne Lazarus, Esq.
Atlanta, Georgia
April 2020

INTRODUCTION

Why I wrote this book

"What in the world were they thinking?" is a question I've frequently asked myself in my forty-plus years in business. What I've learned is that in most cases the answer is simple:

They didn't know any better.

Most stupid mistakes are not due to lack of intelligence – they *are* due to lack of information and/or prior experience, or an ego so big that it thinks it knows everything. Here are some of the mistakes I've witnessed:

- A celebrity went on t.v. to pitch a unique product she created, and didn't have any inventory. When thousands of orders came in, she was left with egg on her face because she had nothing to sell.
- A company with more than two million dollars in annual revenue went belly up because they didn't know anything about basic bookkeeping.
- A CPA embezzled four million dollars from a client by talking him into letting her sign checks.
- A doctor committed suicide because he lost all his savings, as well as his mother's, in an investment scheme that had multiple red flags he ignored.
- A contractor lost all his profit on a "spec" house because he built it over the adjoining property line. As a result, he had to hire surveyors and engineers to re-design all the lots on the entire street in the subdivision to avoid having to tear down the house.

- A retail sales company went out of business because they opened a second shop and failed to keep separate accounting records for the two stores. When sales declined and finances got tight, they had no way to analyze which store was having problems, so they closed both of them.

I've seen lots of good things in business, too:

- The start-up that had a hundred and fifty-thousand dollar profit its first year with more than 75 Google 5-star reviews.
- The start-up that opened business with a thousand dollar investment and was up to five million in revenue in four years.
- The start-up that stuck its neck out and put five thousand dollars in inventory on the shelf before it ran its first ad, and then sold out as soon as the ad ran, making good profits and putting the company on the road to success.
- The start-up that had an attorney draw up its legal documents (contracts for clients and purchase orders for vendors) positioning itself as a professional organization and generating a positive cash flow the first year.

What did these successful start-ups all have in common? Before the first check was written, they hired a bookkeeper. They all went into business to make money, so that's what they took care of right from the start – by establishing an Accounting Department (even if it's only one person, and that person is them).

Poor financial management is one of the primary reasons businesses fail. It can seem a daunting task to maintain the many day-to-day transactions of a company, regardless of its size or the nature of its enterprise. Some companies are what I call "transaction heavy" – for example a retail store might have dozens or even hundreds of transactions every day – but a consultant might only have a few transactions a month; I call these "transaction light." Regardless of the number of transactions, if you don't keep up with them from the get-go, you'll never get a grasp on them. If you are in business, you must know how to handle money.

Although there are a number of bookkeeping processes, I have written this workbook with a focus on Cost Accounting - considered by many accountants to be the most complex of all bookkeeping systems. It is used in construction, manufacturing, food services, clothing factories, and even in hospitals and law firms. Managers always want to know how much profit they make on their customers – whether they are homeowners, clothing buyers, or patients – and cost accounting provides that data.

There are many terms used in Cost Accounting that we're not going to get into since this book is a *primer* and not a full-blown course. However, here is a partial list of some Cost Accounting terms:

- Direct and Indirect costs
- Variable and Fixed costs
- Product and Period costs
- Breakeven Point
- Contribution Margin
- Favorable and Unfavorable Variances
- Full-absorption costing
- Estimated cost
- Differential cost
- Opportunity cost
- Customer acquisition cost

When your business grows to the point where you need all this information, you'll have a full-blown accountant on staff to handle all this for you. In the meantime, be aware that your accounting system is the only way to accurately measure the health of your company.

This workbook is by no means a complete guide to accounting, but, hopefully, it will give you a good foundation on which to build the financial records for your new company, how to handle money, and prevent pitfalls on the path to profits.

Margery Phelps
Marietta, Georgia
April 2020

Making good judgments when one has complete data, facts, and knowledge is not leadership – it's bookkeeping.

-Dee Hock

CHAPTER 1

Cats & Rat

THE BASIC STANDARDS

Before we get started on the nuts and bolts of bookkeeping & accounting, you'll want to know the **basic standards** for handling money and pertinent records. To help you with this, I have a few acronyms.

The first one is: *CATS*

Confidentiality
Accuracy
Timeliness
Security

Confidentiality

The Finance/Accounting department is the only area of your Company that has access to all the records and transactions of every other area of the Company.

It is **absolutely necessary** that anyone with access to your finances maintain the trust of the Company by not ever discussing any financial matter with any other person in the Company, other than those matters which **pertain directly to the other party.** For example:

- Employees and their wages, withholdings, benefits, etc.
- Payments to a Vendor, Subcontractor, or Commissioned Sales personnel

Never ever reveal to another person things such as:

- Amount of cash in the bank (checking, savings, etc.)
- Amounts owed on credit card(s), loan(s), or accounts payable
- Amount of wages or payments to employees, contractors, or commissioned sales personnel

---

Confidentiality is the essence of being trusted.

-Rev. Billy Graham

Accuracy

Because the financial health of a company is measured by its financial records, it is absolutely mandatory that all data entries be accurate. There is no such thing as "approximately" in accounting.

To assure the accuracy of data, certain accounts are "reconciled" at the end of a given period (usually at month-end, although it can vary depending on the account being reconciled). You should **never complete a reconciliation until it is in balance**. Most accounting software does make allowances for unbalanced records by automatically posting the amount that is out of balance to a "Reconciliation Discrepancy" account. **Do not do this!** More on reconciliations on page 57.

> *In math, you are either right or you're wrong.*
>
> -Katherine G. Johnson
> NASA Mathematician

Timeliness

Accounting has numerous deadlines imposed by both the Federal government and the States. Therefore, it is imperative that your accounting records be maintained properly so that timely reports can be issued. Failure to do so can result in penalties and interest being imposed upon your Company. Vendors and subcontractors also have "terms of payment" and the Company can incur late fees and finance charges if bills are not paid timely.

Other items that need timely payment include:

- Rent to landlord
- Car / Truck / Equipment notes payable
- Bank and other business loans
- Utilities

Security

According to the FBI, there were $2.7 Billion in cyber-crimes in 2018 and a survey by the Small Business Administration shows that 88% of small business owners feel threatened by cyber-criminals – but they don't have the financial resources for better IT security. Hopefully, being aware of the dangers of cyber-attacks will help you prevent them. The most common cyber-attacks are:

Malware software designed to damage any facet of your IT; may include ransomware and viruses.

Phishing email or websites with enticing links; when opened, they download damaging code into your system.

Ransomware infects your computer and holds it hostage until you pay the ransom.

Viruses give cybercriminals access to your computer and it spreads to other computers and devices in your system.

WHAT CAN YOU DO? Here's another acronym for you: *SAP*

The Federal Communications Commission (FCC) and Department of Homeland Security (DHS) both have tools to help you Scan, Assess and Plan cybersecurity for your company and they don't cost you anything but your time:

Scan	https://www.us-cert.gov/resources/ncats
Assess	https://www.us-cert.gov/resources/assessments
Plan	https://www.fcc.gov/cyberplanner

PREVENT CYBER ATTACKS

1. Hang "reminder" posters in the workplace and give your employees comprehensive training on
   - Protecting sensitive data on employees, clients and vendors
   - How to identify phishing emails
   - Creating effective passwords
   - Browsing and preventing downloads from suspicious sites
2. Secure your network with a firewall and encryption
3. Use antivirus software; keep it updated with patches and set it to automatically install updates
4. Use multifactor authentication – logons that require multiple id, such as a password and a text code
5. Back-up your data (every day!) and keep the back-up in a secured, off-site location
6. Control access to your computers and data – only highly trusted employees should have Administrative privileges

Securing your checks is also mandatory, so here's what you do for your Checking Account Security Management:

1. All checks must be pre-numbered and used in numerical order.
2. All Wires should be generated by your Accounting Manager and approved by you or your CFO.
3. No checks are to be prepared without proper supporting documentation.
4. Checks are **never** made payable to "Cash" or "Bearer."
5. All checks will include the vendor name as well as their full address.
6. Blank checks are to be kept in a locked and secured location in the Accounting Manager's office.
7. All checks must be accounted for. Void checks are to be defaced and kept for future audits or inspections.
8. All bank accounts will be reconciled monthly by the Accounting Manager and/or Accounting Clerk, and reviewed by you or your CFO.

9. The Accounting Manager must compare the reconciled cash balances to the General Ledger balances and investigate and resolve all variances.
10. The authorized check signature is always by someone other than the person writing the checks. In other words, whoever writes the checks, **NEVER** signs them (unless, of course, the check writer is also the Owner).
11. The mechanical check signer, if applicable, is kept in a locked file cabinet separate from the blank checks and is **NEVER** to be used by the person writing the checks.

Here's one more acronym you should know before we start: *GAAP*

GAAP is ***Generally Accepted Accounting Principles***. Various policy boards in the accounting industry have set standards for recording and reporting accounting information. Although GAAP is not required for all businesses, it is required for publicly traded companies (companies that sell stock to outside investors).

If you want your "small" company to be one of the big players someday, you'd be wise to follow GAAP from the get-go. Besides, if you need a loan, or make an offering to a potential private investor, you want your accounting records (books) to pass muster anyway, so why not do it to begin with. Basically, GAAP requires that accounting data be

RAT

Relevant
Accurate
Timely

Humm….there are those words again – *Accurate* and *Timely*…
Please don't stress out over GAAP. I just wanted you to know about it so you won't be caught with deficient books should the opportunity arise to grow your business, or even sell it on Wall Street.   Since I was mentored for nine years by an

accountant who had been the internal auditor for a Fortune 100 company, that's the standard I learned, and the only way I know.

Basically, GAAP "Accounting standards are the way businesses maintain an overview of their finances"[i] and how the company:

1. Organizes its financial information into accounting records
2. How it summarizes the accounting records on financial statements
3. How it maintains and discloses pertinent financial information

Now that you know some basic standards of the Accounting Department, would you like to learn about *accounting*?

REVIEW:

Why do business owners make mistakes? _____

_____

Define these acronyms:

CATS

    C   _____

    A   _____

    T   _____

    S   _____

GAAP

    G   _____

    A   _____

    A   _____

    P   _____

RAT

    R   _____

    A   _____

    T   _____

CHAPTER 2

Ale

ASSETS, LIABILITIES & EQUITY

The accounting world uses many words you may not be familiar with, so I'm applying another acronym to familiarize you with some basic concepts.

ALE

Assets
Liabilities
Equity

Assets:

What the Company "OWNS"
- Cash in the bank (checking and savings accounts)
- Furnishings (desks, lamps, chairs, filing cabinets, shelving...)
- Computers and other office equipment
- Autos / Trucks / Heavy Equipment
- Accounts Receivable – money due from customers
- Loans Receivable – money the Company has loaned to others
- Advances on Pay – money given to employees, vendors, subcontractors before they have earned it

Liabilities:

What the Company "OWES"
- Loans on Autos / Trucks / Heavy Equipment
- Business loans, bank loans, etc.
- Payables to vendors and subcontractors
- Credit cards
- Lines of Credit (LOC)

Equity:

Equity is the difference between the Assets and the Liabilities and is value of the Owner's interest in the company. In other words, the people who "own" the company have "Equity." There are three types of company owners:

- Stockholders: The owners of a company that is incorporated; we often think of stockholders as the people who own stock in a publicly traded company, but in fact, all incorporated companies are owned by stockholders, even if it just one or a few individuals.

- Owners: Privately held companies. Most small businesses fall into this category.

- Partners: Multiple people own it, but it's not incorporated; many Limited Liability Companies (LLCs) have multiple owners who may, or may not, have equal interest (ownership); Limited Liability Partnerships (LLPs) are, of course, also owned by partners.

Regardless of who *owns* the Company, the value of their ownership (Equity) can be calculated with this formula:

Assets (minus) Liabilities = Equity

The value of your Equity is calculated by the Balance Sheet, which we'll talk about in **Chapter 8.**

Money that the owner(s) pay into and "draw" out of the company are recorded in the Equity Accounts:

- Capital paid in by Owner(s) also called Paid-In-Capital

- Owner's Draws / Stockholder Dividends – the money the Owner withdraws from the company or dividends paid to stockholders

- Retained Earnings: At the end of a reporting period, the Net Income from the Profit & Loss Statement is "transferred" to the Balance Sheet as Retained Earnings. Retained Earnings accumulates on the Balance Sheet for the life of the company.

REVIEW:

Define this acronym and write a description of each word:

ALE

A _____

_____

L _____

_____

E _____

_____

What is the formula to calculate Equity?

_____

CHAPTER 3

RiCE

REVENUE, income, COST OF GOODS SOLD, EXPENSES

Now that we've enjoyed some ALE it's time to have some *RiCE*

Revenue

    and **income**

Cost of Goods Sold (COGS)

Expenses

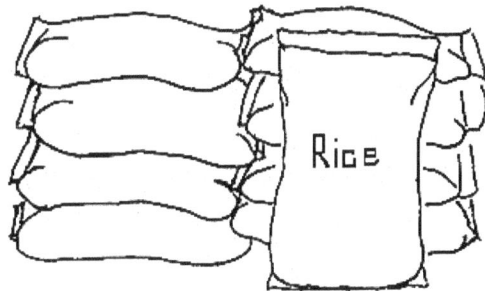

Revenue (and income):

We all go into business to make money. Yes, it's nice to have a "higher purpose" or a "calling" but let's be honest. We want our company to provide us with the financial resources we desire. And that's what revenue is all about – it's the money that flows into your company.

When you provide goods or services to a customer, and they pay you, you have Revenue. Folks often refer to "revenue" as "income" but actually in the accounting world, "income" is what you have after you pay all your expenses (more about this when we talk about Financial Statements in Chapter 8).

Cost of Goods Sold (COGS):

How much does it cost you to provide the goods and services you are providing to your customers? What are the costs directly related to the product you sell?

- What did you pay for the blocks to build a retaining wall for your home repair client?
- How much did you pay a sub-contractor to build that wall?
- How much did you pay for the materials you used to make those shirts you sold in your clothing store?
- How much did you pay for the paper, pens, and computers you sold to customers in your office supply store?
- What was the costs of freight or postage to ship your products directly to customers?

These are all examples of COGS.

Expenses:

In addition to COGS, you will also have lots of other costs related to your business that are not directly related to the customer:

- Rent
- Utilities
- Telephone
- Computers and printers
- Office supplies
- Advertising
- Marketing
- Merchant services (credit card processing fees)
- Salaries for office workers
- Sales commissions

REVIEW:

Define this acronym and write a description of each word: RiCE

R _____

_____

i _____

_____

C _____

_____

E _____

_____

What is the difference between COGS and Expenses?

_____

_____

What is the difference between Revenue and income?

_____

_____

NOTES and QUESTIONS

CHAPTER 4

Building your Financial House

THE CHART OF ACCOUNTS

Now that you have mastered the making of ALE and RiCE, we are going to use them to build the Chart of Accounts for your accounting program. If you were building a house, the first thing you would do is grade (clean-off) the land and then dig holes for the footings. You'd pour concrete into the footings so they would be strong enough to hold up the weight of your house.

The Chart of Accounts is the footing of your company's finances. Everything you do is laid on those accounts, and when you build up data in those accounts, you can create your Financial Reports – consider those the roof of your house.

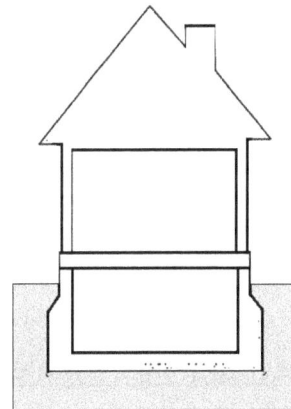

The Chart of Accounts (COA) is a listing of all the account titles (and numbers if you choose to use them) that track your financial transactions. The title of the account should be a brief description of that account's purpose (i.e., Office Supplies – expenditures for paper, pens, clips, calendars, tape, staples...)

The COA has *primary* accounts and *subsidiary* accounts. Here is a typical COA showing the types of accounts and account numbers:

10000 – Assets
20000 – Liabilities
30000 – Equity
40000 – Revenue
50000 – Cost of Goods Sold (COGS)
60000 – Expenses

Notice that each type of account has its own number set: All asset accounts are always series 1000, liabilities are always 2000, etc. (Some companies are so big, and require so many accounts, that they use 10000 and 1000000 as their numbering series.)

Under each of these *primary* accounts are *sub-accounts* to more clearly define the nature of the financial activity in that account, and under the subsidiary account you can have more accounts:

ASSETS

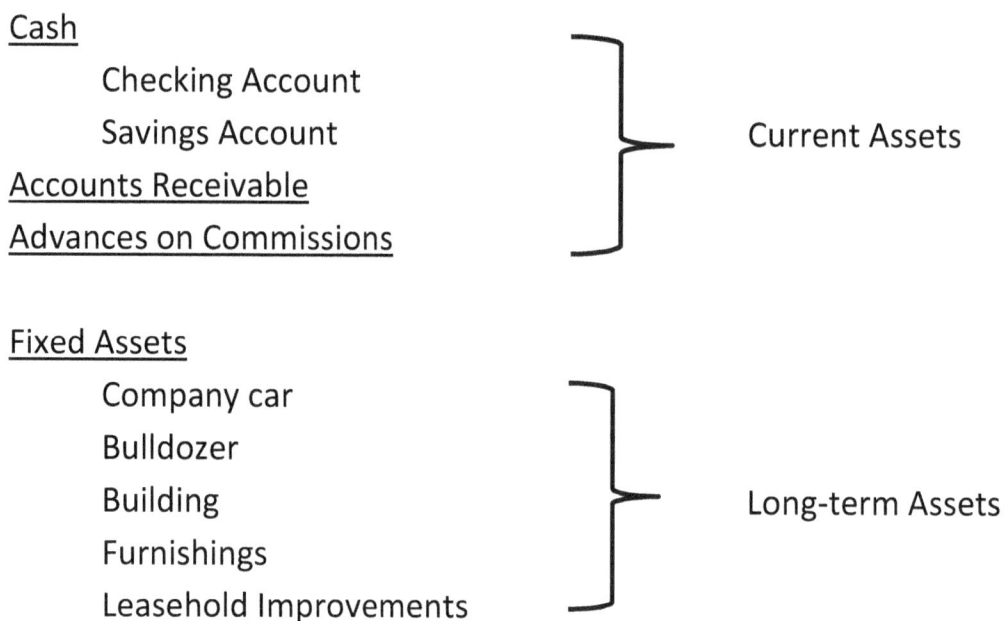

You can see from this list that *current* assets precede *long term* assets. If you need cash in a hurry, look at your current assets to see what you have. If you are going to need cash down the road, you can think about selling a long-term asset, since acquiring that cash will take some time (i.e., such as selling the bulldozer).

WHAT ARE THE ASSETS OF YOUR START-UP COMPANY?

Cash
Investments
Autos/Trucks
Equipment
Computers
Pre-paid rent
Loans
Others

LIABILITIES

<table>
<tr><td>Accounts Payable</td><td rowspan="8">⎫
⎬ Current Liabilities
⎭</td></tr>
</table>

Accounts Payable
Notes Payable
Payroll Taxes Payable
    Fed. w/h
    FICA   **Current Liabilities**
    Medicare
    State w/h
Bank Loan
Auto & Truck notes
    Company car   **Long-term Liabilities**
    Service Truck
Mortgage

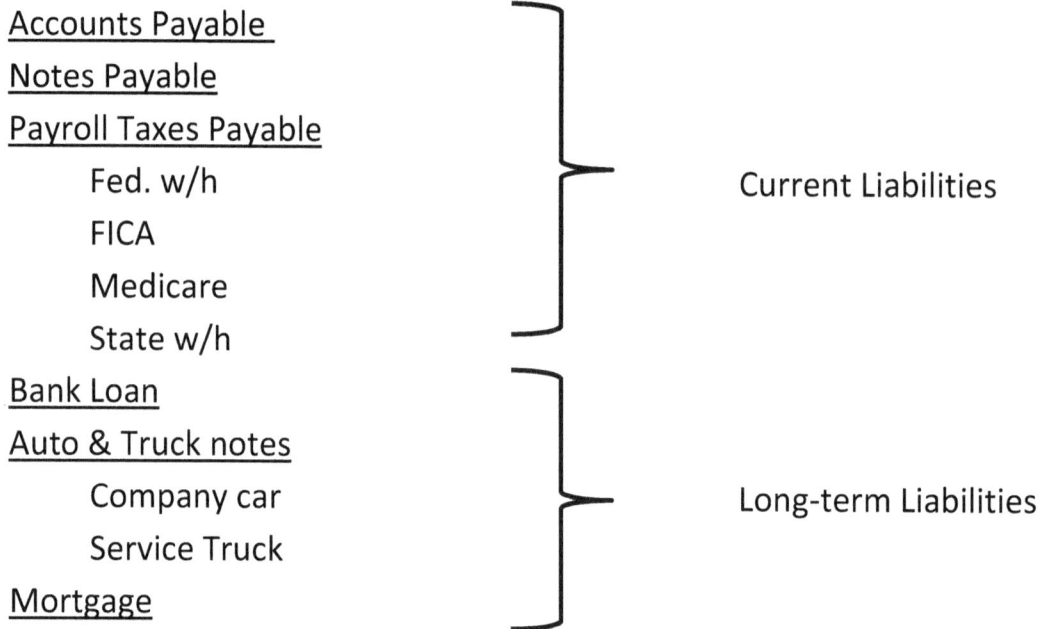

Notice that the Liabilities are listed by *short term* to *long term*, (i.e., current debt precedes long-term accounts).   Here are a few explanations of the above Liability accounts

- Accounts Payable - money owed to vendors/subcontractors for goods and services they provided to your company
- Notes Payable – short term notes that must be paid within one year.
- Payroll Taxes Payable - the amount due for payroll taxes (this includes amounts withheld plus the employer's payroll taxes)
- Bank Loan - the amount to be paid after the next twelve month period. An example would be your start-up funding loan.
- Auto & Truck notes – the amount you owed on the vehicle when you purchased it. This amount is reduced by every payment you make.
- Mortgage on building used in your business (NOT your personal residence)

EQUITY

Paid in Capital
Owner Draws
Retained Earnings

You may prefer to set up your Equity accounts so that the net of what you paid in and withdrew will show on your Balance Sheet. To do it that way, you would have these accounts:

Owner's Equity
Paid in Capital
Owner's Draws

Sweat equity is the most valuable equity there is. Know your business and industry better than anyone else in the world. Love what you do or don't do it.

– Mark Cuban

As we said earlier, Retained Earnings is the account where the Net Income each period flows from the Profit & Loss Statement to the Balance Sheet and is an ongoing accumulation over the life of the company. You'll see how this works when we get to Financial Statements in Chapter 8.

REVENUE

<u>Sales</u>
<u>Services</u>
<u>Reimbursed Expenses</u>

Your company may have more than one *Income Stream*. In other words, you may have revenue from a variety of activities. Since I am a writer and also do accounting, I'll use mine as an example:

REVENUE
- Accounting Services
- Book Sales (for books I sell direct to customers)
- Royalties (book sales from other vendors)

If you have more than one income stream, I can't urge you enough to keep them separate. Down the road you can analyze those revenues to determine if they are worthwhile (profitable) or if you need to let them go. The only way you'll know is to track them separately.

> *If you want to make good financial decisions,*
> *you must have good financial records.*

COST OF GOODS SOLD (COGS)

<u>Materials</u>
<u>Production Labor</u>
<u>Freight</u>

Anything you purchase that will be sold to your customers is included in COGS, and the cost for creating that product is also included since it is direct labor.

For example: A contractor purchases framing lumber, bricks, mortar, roofing shingles, and other supplies to build a house. Then subcontractors are hired to frame the house and install the roof. All these materials are COGS, as well as the labor paid to subcontractors.

COGS also includes inventory - such as clothes a retail store purchases from a wholesaler (or manufacturer) and puts on the shelf for sale to a customer. This type of COGS is quite complicated so we're not going to get into the specifics in this workbook. I did want you to be aware of it because COGS is not "recognized" until the dress or pants are sold. The money spent for "inventory" is carried on the Balance Sheet in a separate Asset account for tracking what you purchased and what was sold.

Inventory includes stuff like FIFO (First in first out), LIFO (Last in first out), Raw Materials, Work in Process (WIP) and Finished Goods. If you are carrying Inventory, please do yourself a favor and hire a bookkeeper who knows how to do this properly.

QuickBooks identifies the things that you *buy* and *sell* as "Items." Please see **Chapter 6 for Items**.

EXPENSES

<u>Advertising & Marketing</u>
      FB ads
      Website
      Signage
<u>Auto Expenses</u>
      Fuel & oil
      Repairs & maintenance
<u>Bank service charges</u>
<u>Insurance</u>
      Auto insurance
      Liability insurance
      Health insurance
<u>Interest and Finance charges</u>
      Auto note interest
      Bank loan interest
<u>Office Supplies</u>
<u>Rent</u>

All your expenses not directly related to your COGS are posted in these accounts, which generally make up the largest section of your COA.

Now that we've talked about the COA, let's create one so you can see what we've done!

CHART OF ACCOUNTS

ASSETS

Current Assets

Cash

Checking Account

Savings Account

Accounts Receivable

Advances on Commissions

Long-term Assets

Fixed Assets

Company car

Bulldozer

Building

Furnishings

Leasehold Improvements

LIABILITIES

Current Liabilities

Accounts Payable

Notes Payable

Payroll Taxes Payable

Fed. w/h

FICA

Medicare

State w/h

Long-term Liabilities

Bank Loan

Auto & Truck notes

Company Car

Service Truck

Mortgage

EQUITY

    Paid in Capital

    Owner Draws

    Retained Earnings

REVENUE

    Sales

    Services

    Reimbursed Expenses

COST OF GOODS SOLD

    Materials

    Production Labor

    Freight

EXPENSES

    Advertising & Marketing

        FB ads

        Website

    Auto Expenses

        Fuel & oil

        Repairs & maintenance

    Bank service charges

    Insurance

        Auto insurance

        Liability insurance

        Health insurance

    Interest and Finance charges

        Auto note interest

        Bank loan interest

    Office Supplies

    Rent

OTHER INCOME

OTHER EXPENSES

WHAT ACCOUNTS DO YOU NEED ON YOUR COA?

Beware of little expenses;
a small leak will sink a great ship.

-Benjamin Franklin

CHAPTER 5

Going Up & Going Down

DEBITS & CREDITS

Accounting uses a technique called *Double-Entry* for recording transactions, which means that there is a "debit" and a "credit" for every posting, and depending on the type of account you are posting to, the balance either goes up or goes down on the debit or credit side of the equation.

If you draw a "T" you can better understand this concept:

ASSETS		LIABILITIES	
DEBITS	CREDITS	DEBITS	CREDITS
Increase	Decrease	Decrease	Increase

Please don't fall into the trap your bank sets for you when they tell you they have "credited" your account because you made a "deposit." Yes, in actuality, on the bank's books, your account is "credited" when you make a deposit because to the bank your account is a "Liability" – it is something the bank "owes" – because that money is yours, not the banks.

On *your* side of the transaction, a deposit to your Cash Account (an Asset) would **increase** on the Debit side. If you write a check, you decrease your Cash Asset with a "credit." Of course, when your bank processes the check you wrote that is a "credit" on your side, the bank will say that they "debited" your account because it reduced the amount they owe you since they paid out that money for that check. This situation can create problems for a start-up business that doesn't understand this critical matter. So again, remember:

> When you make a **deposit** to your bank account, you are making **debit** to your check register.

> When you write a **check** from your Cash (bank) account, you are making a **credit** to your check register.

I hope you have made up your own jingle to remember this:

> *A "D" is a "D"*
> *and a "C" is a "C"*
> *A check is a credit and not a debit*
> *A deposit is a debit and not a credit.*

So, how does an __Equity__ account post debits and credits? Why does it *increase* on the credit side?

EQUITY	
DEBITS	CREDITS
Decrease	Increase

Let's say you are making a deposit of $1000.00 of your own money to set up your new company's checking account. You're making a *deposit* to an Asset account, so it increases on the debit side. Your Equity *Paid in Capital* is therefore increased on the credit side.

	DEBIT	CREDIT
Cash	1000.00	
Paid in Capital		1000.00

But then you decide you need $500 of that money yourself, and you write yourself a company check to *draw* funds from your Equity:

	DEBIT	CREDIT
Draws	500.00	
Cash		500.00

How do we post all that **Revenue** you are receiving from all those big sales your new company is making?

REVENUE	
DEBITS	**CREDITS**
Decrease	Increase

Revenue is a little more complicated. When you make a sale and issue either an **invoice** to a customer (for payment in the future) or a **sales receipt** (when the customer pays you at the time goods are sold), the credit is always to Revenue.

In the case of **a Sales Receipt** for $50.00 (your customer paid you when you sold them that dress), this is the transaction (assuming you deposited the check directly to the company checking account):

	DEBIT	CREDIT
Cash	50.00	
Sales		50.00

Let's say you sold a $2000.00 order for carpet to ABC Consulting and sent them an **Invoice**

	DEBIT	CREDIT
Accounts Receivable	2000.00	
Sales		2000.00

What happens when you receive a check for $2000.00 from ABC for that carpeting you sold to them?

	DEBIT	CREDIT
Accounts Receivable		2000.00
Cash	2000.00	

Now we are down to the **COGS** accounts and how they behave.

COGS	
DEBITS	**CREDITS**
Increase	Decrease

This can be a little more complicated, too, depending on whether you paid cash at the time you purchased the goods, or if you "bought them on account" – meaning you will pay for them later. If you wrote a check to XZY Supplies for $600 at the time of purchase, here's your transaction:

	DEBIT	CREDIT
Materials	600.00	
Cash		600.00

However, if you made the purchase "on account" and received a "bill" from XZY for $600 for those materials, your transaction will record this way:

	DEBIT	CREDIT
Materials	600.00	
Accounts Payable		600.00

So, now you have a "payable" hanging out in your A/P (Accounts Payable) and you write a check to XYZ to pay them:

	DEBIT	CREDIT
Accounts Payable	600.00	
Cash		600.00

Expenses post the same way as COGS:

EXPENSES	
DEBITS	**CREDITS**
Increase	Decrease

The transactions for a "cash" purchase or an "on account" purchase are the same as the COGS transactions.

Lots of new business folks don't take the time to understand *debits* and *credits* and you don't have to worry too much about this. However, having a basic knowledge of double-entry bookkeeping will help you to understand what's going on in the "background" of your accounting software.

When you write a $300 check for rent, your software automatically knows that you are crediting your cash account and debiting your expense account. If you are using software such as QuickBooks for p/c, and you write a check, you can hit **Control – Y** and you will see the actual posting, which will look like this:

	DEBIT	CREDIT
Rent	300.00	
Cash		300.00

You're probably wondering about debits and credits with regard to **CREDIT CARDS** – so please see **Chapter 9** on handling these.

> *Never call an Accountant a credit to his profession;*
> *an Accountant is a debit to his profession.*
>
> -Sir Charles Lyell

CHAPTER 6

What you Buy & What you Sell

ITEMS

All those materials, supplies, and labor you purchase to create the things you sell are identified in QB as **"Items"** and when you set them up, you are essentially creating a subsidiary ledger for tracking all this stuff.

If you have **a Manufacturing Company**, you will purchase a variety of items and then "build" them to create the "finished product" that you sell to your customers. Let's say for example that you are a beverage manufacturing company. Here's some items you would have:

- Glass Bottles
- Aluminum Cans
- Flavoring
- Purified Water
- Caps
- Pull-off Tabs
- Labels

All these *items* would be set up in your **Inventory Account** (Asset) and you would track them by various attributes, such as quarts of purified water, ounces of flavoring, etc. When the product is sold (for example a case of bottled beverages), the costs of inventory items that were sold are subtracted from the Inventory Asset account and added to the appropriate COGS account. In order to sell the "finished goods" the various inventory items have to be "assembled" or "built" – in other words, the bottles are filled with beverage and flavoring, a label is attached, and the bottle is capped.

These **"inventory builds"** can be rather complicated, so if you are in the manufacturing arena, be sure to hire a competent bookkeeper to set this up and maintain it for you. Believe me, it is well worth your cost to do this properly from the start.

Another type of *item* are those for **Retail Sales**. In this instance, let's say you are a small clothing store, your items might be:

- Blue Blouses – Sizes 2, 4, 8, 10
- Red Jeans – Sizes 10, 12, 14
- Purple Scarves – no size
- Shawls – Sizes S, M, L, XL

Each of the above items will have its own **SKU** (Stock-Keeping-Unit) and, like our bottled beverage, when it is sold, it is subtracted from Inventory Asset and added to COGS. It's prudent for any company selling products to invest in a good POS (Point-of-Sale) software to track the incoming inventory as well as the sales to customers and the applicable sales taxes.

A **Construction Company** will have an entirely different list of items but unlike manufacturing and retail, which carry the initial item costs on the Inventory Asset account, the purchased items are posted directly to the appropriate COGS account. The exception would be a home manufacturer who is building a quantity of houses and then selling them, in which case they would be inventoried.

If a construction-related company does limited work (for example a roofing company), they can set up their own items for tracking products bought and sold. However, for a General Contractor, who provides items and services in all areas of construction, I highly recommend the "Schedule of Values" as set by the American Institute of Architects (AIA). This gives a general contractor every possible item they could use in their company. In many instances it is also compatible with requirements of owners and their bankers who are funding the construction of the house, commercial building, warehouse, etc.

Some companies may have only a few items. For example, a **Consultant** might have:

- Fees
- Travel Reimbursements
- Postage Reimbursements
- Gas Allowance
- Mileage Allowance

A **Contractor** who only does one job – for example a ceramic tile installer – would also have limited items. If that contractor is providing labor only, and not any materials, he might have items such as:

- Ceramic Floor Tile Install @ $xxx / sq. ft.
- Porcelain Wall Tile Install @ $xxx/ sq. ft.

Each company has its own individual needs, so before you set up your *items* in your accounting software, think about what exactly you will be providing in the way of materials and labor, and what you will be charging your customer for those items.

Money is a tool. Used properly, it makes something beautiful; used wrong, it makes a mess.

-Bradley Vinson

WHAT ARE THE "ITEMS" YOU NEED TO SET UP?

CHAPTER 7

Data Diary

THE GENERAL LEDGER

When you mix ALE and RiCE, the COA, and Debits and Credits, you have a diary of all the data in your accounting records - The General Ledger. This is where all transactions are posted and tracked, and it is a permanent record of your company's business transactions.

In the past, the G/L was used only for ALE, and all other transactions were kept in "subsidiary" ledgers. However, today's accounting software for small businesses generally has one ledger since technology has made it possible to have sub-accounts of primary accounts.

The G/L will have the following **data columns for each account** on your COA. The G/L also follows the exact order of your COA, with your bank accounts first, followed by other Assets, then Liabilities, Equity accounts, COGS, and Expenses.

ACCOUNT NAME
1. Date
2. Reference or Transaction #, Check #, Bill #, Invoice #
3. Name: Vendor/Contractor, Employee, Customer
4. Debit
5. Credit
6. Balance: This is a running balance of all the debits & credits posted to the account

When your accounting software pulls the data for a report, it selects the balance in the applicable G/L accounts for the date of your report. This allows you to have reports by day, week, month, or year, and any multiple of those time frames.

The Trial Balance, which we will discuss on page 48, is simply a summary of the **balances** in each account on you G/L on the day of your report.

In order to have valid and verifiable data in your G/L, postings to your various accounts and subsidiary accounts should be made from the **business document directly related to the transaction**. For example:

You receive a bill from a vendor - you post it with the following as shown on that bill:

1. Date on the bill (NOT the date you entered it)
2. Due date (as indicated on the bill – if terms, post that, such as "Net 10 days")
3. Bill # (they have probably used *invoice #*) (accounting software may identify this as *Reference #)*
4. Vendor Name (be sure you spell it correctly)
5. Amount of bill
6. Customer or Job if applicable

You purchased job supplies from Home Depot on your Amex card - you post the credit card receipt with the following as shown on that receipt:

1. Date on the receipt
2. Vendor name
3. Amount
4. When you post a credit card receipt, be sure to also post it to the appropriate customer job, if applicable

In other words, **everything you post needs documentation**. If you ever get audited and you don't have your back-up documents, IRS can disallow those expenses related to transactions that have no documentation.

Accounting software makes it possible for you to drill down to the complete history of a transaction. In QB for p/c, click *Control – H*. If you have a bill from Vendor ABC, you will be able to find the original bill and how it was posted and any applicable payments you made on that bill. If that expense was also invoiced to a customer, you will see that, too.

Control-H can be a very useful tool. If you are in QB On-Line, use the search icon (magnifying glass) and enter the amount and it will do the same.

If you need to run a report of your G/L, be sure there is plenty of paper in your printer because this report will be the biggest one in your accounting software. Also, due to the size, it's usually better to set it up to print "landscape" rather than "portrait" to capture all those columns of data across one sheet.

The G/L gives you detailed data on all your company's financial transactions; please be sure your postings are complete and accurate, and your G/L will give you valid information about your business operations.

Who led the accounts into battle?
General Ledger.

-TheBig4Accountant Tweet 6/10/19

Great things in business are never done by one person.
They're done by a team of people.

-Steve Jobs

CHAPTER 8

Fiscal Facts

THE FINANCIAL STATEMENTS

There are numerous accounting reports but the main four are the

- Balance Sheet
- Profit & Loss Statement (also called Income Statement)
- Trial Balance
- Cash Flow

The **Balance Sheet** is the report that summarizes all the data in **ALE** and shows the health of your company at a specific point in time. Also known as *Statement of Financial Position*, the Balance Sheet is a report of your Assets, Liabilities, and Equity so you can assess your company's ability to meet its obligations.

Note that the date on the Balance Sheet is for one given day, not a period such as a month or a year, as you will see on the Profit & Loss Statement below. Also, you'll see that the Net Income shown on the Balance Sheet for December 31, 2021 is $ 12,696 – the exact same amount as shown on as the Net Income on the P&L Statement for the period ending December 31, 2021.

Note also that the total for Assets must equal the amount of your Liabilities PLUS your Equity. If these numbers don't match, you have a problem.

Here's a sample:

Balance Sheet for ABC Company				
December 31, 2021				
ASSETS			**LIABILITIES**	
Current Assets			Current Liabilities	
Checking Account	1,000		Accounts Payable	9,000.00
Accounts Receivable	12,000		Credit Cards	1,000.00
Total Current Assets	**13,000**		Total Current Liabilities	**10,000.00**
Fixed Assets			Long Term Liabilities	90,000.00
Building	100,000		**TOTAL LIABILITIES**	**100,000.00**
Truck	4,000		**EQUITY**	
Total Fixed Assets	**104,000**		Paid in Capital	1,000
			Retained Earnings	3,304
			Net Income	12,696
			TOTAL EQUITY	17,000
TOTAL ASSETS	**117,000**		**TOTAL LIABILITIES & EQUITY**	117,000

Information on the Balance Sheet is critical to knowing your **Working Capital** which can be defined **as *the available funds you have to handle your current liabilities*.** It is computed with this formula:

Current Assets – Current Liabilities = Working Capital

In the above Balance Sheet, the numbers in the working capital formula would be:

13,000 - 10,000 = 3,000.

This indicates you have sufficient funds to pay your current liabilities.

The **ratio** of your working capital is also important and is computed as

Current Assets ÷ Current Liabilities = Working Capital Ratio

Based on our Balance Sheet, the ratio would be: 13,000 ÷ 10,000 = 1.3.

Generally, 1.5 is a good working capital ratio, but above 2.0 is not necessarily better. If the ratio is below 1.0, the company probably has liquidity problems. Financial analysts have differing opinions, but generally a ratio of 1.1 to 2 indicates that your company has healthy working capital, that you are handling cash wisely, and are a low risk for defaulting on your bills. If your ratio is less than 1.0, it generally indicates that you would have trouble paying off your short-term liabilities, and this may not bode well down the road.

The importance of working capital cannot be overstated. If a business is to thrive, it must have a happy relationship between current assets and current liabilities.

> *The primary objective of financial reporting is to provide information useful for decision making.*
>
> -Financial Accounting Standards Board

The **Profit & Loss Statement** is all about your **RiCE** and shows you how much your company earned (Revenue) and how much it spent (COGS plus Expenses) and the amount of your Net Income.

Since we all use accounting software to handle our bookkeeping, you don't need to worry about creating these financial reports. Your system will do it for you. It's important, however, to know how all these numbers interact to give you the data you need to make important business decisions. For example:

> A start-up company budgeted $6,000 for its advertising and marketing the first three months in operation and the gross income from these endeavors was $12,000, with a net income of $2,000. The president decided that the return on his advertising/marketing budget was good, so in the next nine months he doubled his investment in this segment of

his business. Guess what happened? His gross income tripled! And his Net Income went way up, too.

Why was he able to take such a gamble on advertising & marketing? Because he had the data to show him that it was working – it was making him money. And with all that extra money, he was able to hire more employees.

As shown on our COA (pages 25 and 26) and the above Profit & Loss Statement, we have two accounts that need further explanation:

OTHER INCOME

This account holds the revenue transactions that are not normal to your day-to-day business operations and includes things such as:

- Interest earned on a savings account
- Monies from the sale of an asset
- Rent from a sub-lease of your office space

OTHER EXPENSES

Like other income, these expenses are for transactions that are not part of your daily business, and includes:

- Loss on the sale of asset
- Cost of currency exchange

Let's take a look at the Profit & Loss Statement for ABC Company for the year 2021:

Profit & Loss Statement ABC Company January 1, 2021 to December 31, 2021	
Income	
Sales	50,000
Services	10,000
Reimbursed Expenses	2,000
Total Income	**62,000**
Cost of Goods Sold	
Materials	20,000
Labor	15,000
Freight	700
Total COGS	**35,700**
GROSS PROFIT	**26,300**
Expenses	
Advertising & Marketing	
FB Ads	1,100
Website	1,500
Total Advertising & Marketing	**2,610**
Auto Expenses	
Fuel & oil	1,900
Repairs & maintenance	550
Total Auto Expenses	**2,450**
Bank Service Charges	24
Insurance	
Auto Insurance	1,200
Liability Insurance	1,350
Total Insurance	**2,550**
Office Supplies	1,220
Rent	3,600
Total Expense	**12,454**
Net Ordinary Income	**13,846**
Other Income and Expense	
Loss on Sale of Company Truck	(1,200)
Dividend Income	50
Net Other Income/Expense	**(1,150)**
NET INCOME	**12,696**

The Income Statement is used by a variety of groups who want to evaluate a business and its activities:

- Investors – determine the investment worthiness of the company
- Creditors – consider the risk of making loans to the company
- IRS – impose taxes
- Owners – make decisions on the operation of the company

Remember those debits and credits we talked about? Your **Trial Balance** is a report that gives you the either the debit or the credit balance in each of your General Ledger accounts. When you total each column, they must be equal. Here's a sample Trial Balance:

Trial Balance XYZ Products Company December 31, 2021		
ACCOUNT	**DEBIT**	**CREDIT**
Checking Account	50,000	
Savings Account	16,000	
Accounts Receivable	5,000	
Fixed Assets	125,000	
Accounts Payable		2,500
Mortgage Payable		90,000
Owner's Equity		93,000
Sales		200,000
COGS	125,000	
Advertising & Marketing	5,000	
Auto Expenses	6,000	
Insurance	7,000	
Office Supplies	300	
Payroll Expenses	12,000	
Rent	30,000	
Utilities	4,200	
TOTALS	**385,500**	**385,500**

After posting and reconciling all your accounts, you should run a *Trial Balance* to be sure everything is in balance before you print your other financial reports. If the trial balance is off, the other reports are, too, and you need to find the problem.

The **Cash Flow Statement** is the last of our major financial statements and may be more difficult to understand. Basically, this report looks at three different areas of the company:

- Operations
- Investing
- Financing

The Cash Flow Statement is a mandatory report required by the Securities and Exchange Commission (SEC) for all publicly traded companies. Although start-ups don't fall into this category, understanding this report, and the data it provides, can help you with your small business.

As you might surmise from the title *Cash Flow Statement*, this report summarizes the flow of cash into and out of your company in a given period. You will always want to have more cash flowing into your business than out of it. If more cash flows out than flows in, you won't be able to meet your financial obligations.

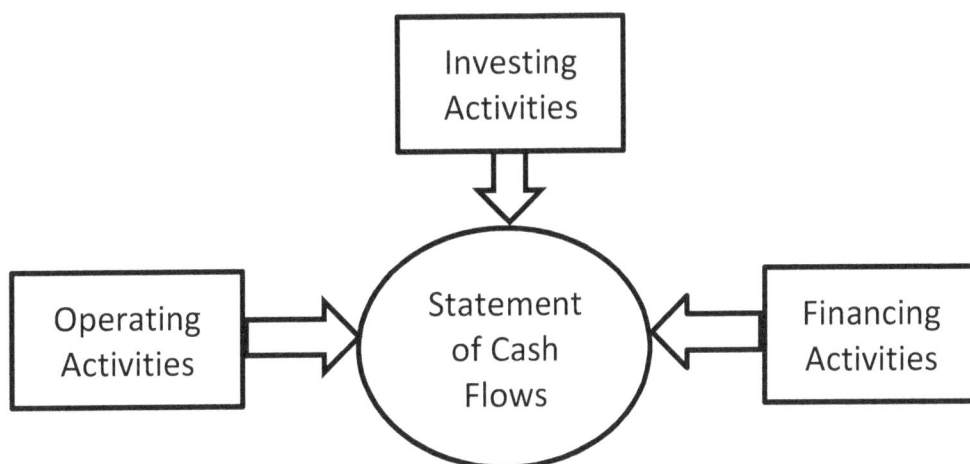

There are two methods of calculating cash flow – Direct and Indirect. QuickBooks provides a Cash Flow report, as do other accounting software programs.

Whenever a company receives a large influx of cash, it can be very tempting to the owner to take that cash for personal use. I've seen this happen numerous times during my forty years in accounting and the result has always been bad.

Here are two examples:

> A company owner received an unexpected $25,000 royalty payment. As the bookkeeper, I was greatly relieved because the cash flow was tight, and this inflow was a life-line. However, rather than leaving the windfall in the company hoppers, the owner withdrew it for personal use. The company never recovered from its tight cash flow situation and went out of business. That 25K could have saved it.
>
> In the second situation, a nutritional products start-up received tens of thousands of dollars from investors. Rather than invest the money in marketing and inventory, the owner took his girlfriend on some expensive trips. I don't have to tell you what happened to them.

If you treat your company as you would your child, and set aside cash for its future, you will be richly rewarded by a company that will continue to provide for you many years down the road. I've seen this time and time again with many successful companies. I hope your company will be one of them.

CHAPTER 9

The Handy Money Tool

CREDIT CARDS

We all know how handy it is to use our credit cards. They also help us build credit and offer enticing rewards. But accounting for them can be complicated, so we're giving **Credit Cards** their own chapter.

First, a credit card is a Liability – the balance you owe on your credit card is on your Balance Sheet, under your *Current Liabilities*. If you have more than one credit card, you should have a *primary* Credit Card account, with each individual credit card listed as a sub-account:

> **LIABILITIES**
> > Current Liabilities
> > > Credit Cards
> > > - American Express *0001
> > > - Bank of America * 0002
> > > - Chase Bank * 0003

If you have this situation, with multiple credit cards, please be sure when you post a credit card transaction that you post it to the correct credit card account!! Do not post it to the general "credit cards" account.

Second, a *purchase* on a credit card, is a debit to one of these accounts:

- Expenses
- COGS
- Accounts Payable

Let's look at some "T" transactions to show you how we use credit cards. For these examples, we will use your Amex *0001 account.

1.   **Expenses:**   Pay your expenses "on the spot" with your Amex * 0001 card for things such as

- McDonalds - Meal   (25.00)
- RaceTrac- Gas (40.00)
- Office Depot - Supplies (10.00)
- Delta - Airline tickets (300.00)

375.00

Your "T" transactions would look like this:

	DEBIT	CREDIT
Meals	25.00	
Amex		25.00
Gas	40.00	
Amex		40.00
(etc.)		

As a result of these transactions, your *expense* accounts all increased, and so did your Amex, so now you owe Amex 375.00 for these four purchases.

2.   **COGS:**   Pay your COGS "on the spot" for things such as

- Home Depot - Supplies (200.00)
- Lowe's - Materials (50.00)
- FedEx - Freight (15.00)

265.00

Your "T" transaction would be the same as Expenses except you have increased your COGS accounts and also increased your Amex *0001 by 265.00.

3.   **Accounts Payable:**   Most accounting software allows you to pay accounts with your credit card if you have set it up for this function. Let's say you owe ABC Supply company 1,000.00 on account, and it's sitting in you're A/P folder awaiting payment. You open your "Pay Bills" function, select ABC Supply, pay 1,000.00 by Amex. The transaction would decrease your A/P and increase your Amex and the transaction would look like this:

DEBIT	CREDIT
A/P 1000.00	Amex 1000.00

As a result of paying vendor ABC Supply with your Amex, you have reduced your A/P and increased the amount you owe Amex. Now the balance in your Amex account is 1,640.00 as shown on your General Ledger:

AMEX * 0001

NAME	DEBIT	CREDIT	BALANCE
McDonald's		25.00	25.00
RaceTrac		40.00	65.00
Office Depot		10.00	75.00
Delta		300.00	375.00
Home Depot		200.0	575.00
Lowe's		50.00	625.00
FedEx		15.00	640.00
ABC Supply		1,000.00	1,640.00

You receive a statement from Amex, and it shows you owe them 1,640.00 with a due date of February 1. **DO NOT** post this as a payable bill!! The amount of 1,640.00 is already on your account, hanging out in the Amex register. If you post this as a bill, you will be overstating your liabilities (your A/P) by 1,640.00!!

You have two options to pay Amex:

1. Log into your on-line Amex account and pay the 1,640.00.
   Make note of the payment confirmation number.
   Open your "write checks" function and enter the payment to Amex for 1,640.00. Enter confirmation # on the ref. line.
   a. The check is Payable to American Express
   b. The account paid is Amex *0001
   c. There is no check number

2. Open your "write check" function
   a. The check is Payable to American Express
   b. The account paid is Amex *0001
   c. On ref. line enter your full account number
   d. Print a live check
   e. Sign and mail it to Amex.

As a result, your payment transaction "T" account would look like this:

	DEBIT	CREDIT
Amex	1,640.00	
Cash		1,640.00

(Remember, checks you write are *credits* to your checking account.)

The balance you owe Amex is now -0- because you paid the account in full and your Amex register looks like this:

NAME	DEBIT	CREDIT	BALANCE
Lowe's		50.00	625.00
FedEx		15.00	640.00
ABC Supply		1,000.00	1,640.00
Amex	1,640.00		0.00

From time to time you may receive a "credit" on your Amex account when you return an item to a store. Let's suppose you are returning 500.00 in Lumber to Home Depot for a Supplies Expense that you purchased on Amex. Depending on your accounting software, there are different ways to post this:

- In QB for p/c, open the "post credit card" function and click on the "credit" button, and then proceed to post the transaction.
- In QB On-Line, open the " + " window to add a transaction, select "credit card credit" and post the transaction.

Either way, your "T" would look like this:

	DEBIT	CREDIT
Amex	500.00	
Supplies		500.00

This would result in a *credit* to the applicable expense account for the return and a *debit* to your Amex account. You have reduced your Supplies expense account by 500.00 since you returned the lumber, and you have reduced the amount you owe Amex account because of that return.

WHAT CREDIT CARD ACCOUNTS DO YOU HAVE?

Do you have questions about using and posting credit cards?

> *A credit card is a money tool, not a supplement to money.*
>
> -Paula Nelson

CHAPTER 10

Matching Monies

RECONCILIATIONS

You keep your records *in balance* and accurate by regular **reconciliation** of various accounts. In other words, the monies recorded in your accounting software MUST match the monies shown on financial statements you receive from banks and other "outside" sources. It may seem a daunting task, but it is actually quite simple if all your postings are correct.

You can expect to receive monthly statements on the following accounts, and they should be reconciled in a timely manner:

- Bank checking accounts
- Bank savings accounts
- Credit card accounts
- Auto loans
- Equipment loans
- Bank loans
- Lines of credit
- Mortgages on company owned buildings

The procedure is basically the same for each, and the only variable will be the number of transactions to be reconciled in a given period. A checking account or credit card might have a hundred or more transactions, whereas a mortgage, bank loan, or auto loan will only have a few. Regardless of the account to be reconciled, this is what you need to do:

1. Open the reconciliation window in your accounting software.
    a. In QB for p/c open *Bank* tab, go down to *Reconcile* and open the drop-down for the account to be reconciled.
    b. In QB On-Line, open the *Accounting* tab, select *Reconcile* and open from the drop-down the account you want to reconcile.
2. Enter the statement's *Ending Date* and the *Ending Balance* as shown on the statement.
3. Be sure the *Beginning Balance* in your accounting program is exactly the same as shown on the statement. If this is the first statement you have reconciled on this account, the beginning balance will be -zero-.
4. Enter the *Bank fees* or *Interest* earned in the appropriate windows. These amounts are shown on your statement.
5. The reconciliation window will open, and you should check off each item in the window that matches the items on the statement.
6. When the *reconciled balance* is -Zero- this means that the debits and credits on your account match the statement.
7. Click on the *Finish* reconcile to complete.
8. Reconciliation Reports will appear for you to print and attach to your statement. Rather than printing, I archive them in my computer and write a large "R" in the upper right-hand corner of the statement to let me know that it is reconciled.

That wasn't so bad, was it? One word of caution: **DO NOT** delete a reconciled transaction. If you do, the next time you start to reconcile that account, the beginning balance will be off. This can be very cumbersome to fix.

Only Accountants can save the world

through peace, good will, and reconciliations.

-Sayingspoint.com

CHAPTER 11

Is it a Bill or is it an Invoice?

PAYABLES & RECEIVABLES

When a vendor/subcontractor sends you their "invoice" you have received a **"Bill."**

When you "bill" a customer, you have sent them an **"Invoice."**

In other words, a "bill" is something that the Company "owes" and an "invoice" is something that is "owed to" the Company.

PAYABLES

Most of the goods and services (such as contract labor) that you purchase will be on credit. In other words, you will pay for them at a later date, and they are referred to as *Accounts Payable (*A/P*)*. Other financial obligations, such as salaries and payroll taxes, are reported as separate liabilities and are NOT included in A/P.

To stay on top of your payables (remember – *timeliness)* bills should be posted as soon as they are received so that you don't incur late fees or finance charges for delinquent payment. When you receive a bill, you should:

1. Review vendor data to ensure that bill hasn't already been paid.

2. Run calculator to be sure that computations and total on bill are correct.

3. Code the bill using the Chart of Accounts or Applicable "Item" and any other document provided.

4. Enter (post) the invoice into Accounts Payable. **Always** enter the vendor's invoice number when you post and write a brief reference to the job on the appropriate line, and post the "terms" or due date. In QB-On-Line, click the (+) tab, go to the Vendors section, and click "add bill." In QB for p/c open "Vendors" and select "add bill."

5. Make a "posting" mark on the bill. This is usually a "P" surrounded by a circle. You should get in the habit of always putting your posting mark in the same area on bills. That way, you can easily recognize a "posted bill" and not enter it again.

6. File the posted bills and supporting documentation in the "open" A/P file by Vendor Name and *DUE DATE*, if not being paid at that time.

When you are ready to pay a bill, **ALWAYS** pay if from the "Bill Pay" function in your accounting software. If you just write them a check, that check won't be "attached" to that payable and it will still be hanging out in your A/P.

1. Open "Bill Pay" and select the vendor(s) you want to pay. If you have posted a credit memo, apply that credit to the bill. For example, if you have a $100 bill from ABC Supply, and you also have a $25 credit, the amount of your check will be $75.

2. Print the check to the vendor and attach the bottom portion of the check voucher to the paid bill. Mail the check to the vendor with the voucher attached so that they will know what you are paying. (A sample voucher check is shown on the next page.)

3. The lower/2nd voucher is stapled to the paid bill and filed in the vendor's file. **Do NOT put paid vendor bills in a Job file**. Every vendor should have their own file and all activity related to that vendor should be in that folder, **NOT** a job folder.

Check with (2) vouchers ──────────▶

It's worth the cost of voucher checks when you consider the convenience they provide. Also, order your checks with the security hologram; they are designed to prevent fraud. I had a client who used only cheap checks and they were the frequent target of check fraud criminals because their checks were so easily copied.

RECEIVABLES

Accounts Receivable (A/R) probably account for the major portion of your company's liquid assets and you should be diligent about not only collecting these monies, but also in how you handle them when received. Daily recording and depositing funds received can greatly impact your cash flow, and the monitoring of receivables can help you minimize losses from accounts that are uncollectible.

Let's say your customer, Jane Jones, has sent you a check to pay the invoice you sent to her. This is what you do:

1. **YOU MUST** record that check to Jane's account by opening the "Payment" window, selecting Jane Jones, and applying her payment to the invoice. **DO NOT** simply deposit the check <u>without posting the payment</u> to Jane's account. You can't begin to imagine how screwed your books will be if you do that.

2. When you post Jane's check, be sure to enter the date received, NOT the date on the check. Also enter her check number. If this is the only check you are depositing, the "deposit" window will be to your bank account.

3. However, *if you are depositing multiple check payments* from multiple customers, record each payment on each customer's register, but the "deposit" window should be **"Undeposited Funds."**

4. After you record all the checks, open the "Deposit" function, then select the checks from "Undeposited" funds that you are depositing. All the customer payments you received will be on that list of *Undeposited Funds* if you did it correctly.

5. I always like to count the number of checks I have and confirm the amount of each check against the checks shown in the window. Make sure you select the correct bank to which you are making the deposit, then click "save" and close.

6. Be sure to take the checks to your bank the same day or do your electronic deposit, or if you use an iPhone ap, make the deposit that way.

7. If you do deposit via your phone ap, put a check-mark or some identifying note on each check so you'll know that you have deposited it.

8. Put the check(s) that you deposited via your phone ap in your *Deposits* file so you'll have them if there is a problem with your bank reconciliation.

Please don't put your business in jeopardy by ignoring your A/R. Put a system in place that:

- Sends timely invoices to customers
- Sends "friendly" reminders if payment is not received by your due date
- Provides a debt collection system for delinquent accounts
- Monitors customers who only make partial payments
- Prevents you from sending another order to a customer who is behind on their payments

If you have an extensive number of customers on credit and a significant A/R, you should consider regular review of your **DSO – Days Sales Outstanding**. Here is the formula for this computation:

$$DSO = Accounts\ Receivable \div Total\ Credit\ Sales\ x\ \#\ Days$$

Select a period (such as one month) and pull the A/R and Total Credit Sales data for that period and divide A/R by the # of sales, then multiply by the number of days in that period. If your DSO is low, you should be in good shape; however, a large DSO can indicate that it's taking too long to collect your money.

When it comes to Accounts Receivable remember this: It's your money. Don't feel guilty for collecting it.

Some people dream of success, while other people
get up every morning and make it happen.

-Wayne Huizenga, Founder of AutoNation

CHAPTER 12

Fixing the Numbers

JOURNAL ENTRIES & ADJUSTING JOURNAL ENTRIES

You'll hear the terms *Journal Entry* and *Adjusting Journal Entry* and because there are two phrases for essentially the same function, I thought you could use my explanation.

A ***Journal Entry*** (J/E) is done when you need to get data on your books and there is no other way to record it. These J/Es can occur on any day and are not limited to a specific time, such as the close of a monthly or yearly accounting period. Here are some examples of a J/E:

1. Cash-back earned on a credit card
2. Property tax payment made from your mortgage escrow account
3. Purchase of a new asset with trade-in and loan

#1: Let's say you receive your Discover card statement and have earned $15 which you want to apply immediately to your current balance of $1,000. This $15 is not only **other income** you need to recognize on your books, it can also be used for various activities, such as paying down your balance or purchasing a gift card.

You decide to pay down the balance on your account and make that transaction on-line, noting the confirmation number. Next, open your accounting software. In QB On-line, go to (+), click Journal Entry. In QB for p/c, go to *Company*, then click on *Make General Journal Entries*. Be sure that the date on your J/E is the same date as your transaction. Enter the confirmation number of your on-line transaction in the *Description* so that you'll have it should you need it in the future.

For either software, here's your entry:

	DEBIT	CREDIT
Discover Card	15.00	
Other Income		15.00

You can see from this transaction, you have decreased the amount you owe Discover by $15, since that is a liability account, and it decreases on the debit side, and you have also increased your Other Income by $15, since that is a revenue account which increases on the credit side. You have now properly accounted for the increased income and reduced liability although no "cash" was involved.

#2: You want to record the $300 payment of your property taxes by your escrow account:

	DEBIT	CREDIT
Property tax	300.00	
Escrow Account		300.00

In this situation, you have properly recognized the $300 property tax expense because your expenses increase on the debit side; your escrow account, which is an Asset, has been reduced by $300, since assets decrease on the credit side. Again, there was no "cash" involved in the transaction.

#3: In our third example for a J/E, you purchased a new car ($30,000), traded in an old car ($10,000), paid off the old auto loan ($2,000) and took out a new car loan ($23,850) and had some related expenses, all displayed on the Bill of Sale. This is more complicated as shown here:

	DEBIT	CREDIT
New Car (Asset)	30,000	
Old Car (Asset)		10,000
New car tag (Expense)	50	
New car ins. (Expense)	300	
Sales tax (Expense)	1,500	
Old Car loan payoff (Lia)	2,000	
New Car loan (Lia)		23,850
TOTALS	33,850	33,850

(Humm...debits and credits are starting to make sense now, aren't they? Also, notice that Debits and Credits for every J/E must be equal.)

In this situation you have added the new car to your assets and taken the old car off. You have also recognized the expenses related to the purchase of the new car, paying off the old car loan, and the new car loan balance.

In the three situations above, there is no "accounting period" restriction on the date of the entries. They are simply dated the day on the Bill of Sale.

An ***Adjusting Journal Entry*** is done at the end of a specific of time, such as the end of a month, a fiscal quarter, or year. Examples of AJEs:

- Expenses accrued but not yet paid
- WIP (Work in Process)
- Inventory Adjustments
- Depreciation
- Allowance for doubtful accounts
- Year-end adjustments to bring books in balance with tax return

These types of journal entries are generally prepared by your CPA and given to your bookkeeper (or you) to post. They can be even more complicated than our #3 J/E above. Since these are all related to a specific period, it is absolutely essential that the date entered is exactly the same as the date given by your CPA.

Journal entries are one more tool in your bookkeeping barn where you keep that ALE, the RiCE, those CATS, the RAT, the SAP, and GAAP. With all these tools, you are sure to grow a prosperous business.

> *The word accounting comes from the word accountability.*
> *If you are going to be rich, you need to be accountable for your money.*
>
> -Robert Kiyosaki

CHAPTER 13

Watching every Penny

OTHER FINANCIAL REPORTS

You'll have better control over the financial health of your company if you do a regular review of overall business operations. Reports such as these will help you in your analysis:

1. Customer Acquisition Cost
2. Job Costs / Item costs as a percentage of Income
3. Revenue by Customer
4. Expenses by Vendor
5. Aging Payables and Receivables
6. Budget v. Actual
7. Forecasts

#1: **Customer Acquisition Cost (CAC)** If you spend more to acquire a customer than you earn from them, you are upside down. With the CAC, you will have the information to help you make decisions such as:

- How much can you spend to acquire a customer?
- Which type of customer is best for your company?
- How many sales reps do you need to hire?

According to HubSpot[ii], the average CAC can range from a low of $7 for the travel industry up to $395 for technology/software.[iii] Here's the formula to determine your company's CAC:

(Total Sales + Marketing Expenses) ÷ (Number of New Customers) = CAC

When you pull these numbers from your accounting data, the values should come from a specific period. In other words, in one month you spent $1000 on sales, $2000 on marketing (including ads) and you acquired 50 new customers:

$$3,000 \div 50 = 60 \text{ CAC}$$

Let's say those 50 customers generated $20,000 in sales:

$$20,000 \div 50 = 400 / \text{Avg. Revenue per Customer}$$

This tells you that you spent $60 to earn $400 gross per customer. That looks like a pretty good return on your investment.

#2: Job and Item Costs as a Percentage of Income   Your accounting software provides a variety of reports that allow you to set various defaults for percentages of gross income, net income, total expenses, etc., and you would be wise to use them. Every time I set up a new job for a client, I also create the Job Costs reports which will populate once the data is entered. This can help you make decisions such as:

- Type of Job that is profitable
- Item profitability

Let's look at some examples:

You are a contractor and do bathroom and kitchen remodeling and you also do new build projects such as porches and decks You track all your costs for labor and materials for each type of job. In assessing them you discover that your profit margin is higher for the decks and porches than the remodeling. You might want to start focusing your marketing efforts on the more profitable portions of your business.

The same holds true for your purchases of materials and the income each finished good provides, as well as the labor. Which suppliers and subcontractors give you the best profit margin?

#3: Revenue by Customer   Let's face it – some customers are really wonderful, pay you on time, never complain, and give you good Google ratings. Others are just a plain ole pain in the neck. Sometimes the most difficult customers are also the most profitable. Determining who to "hold onto" and who to "let go" can only be determined when you look at the overall value of that customer.

In addition, the revenue and net income by customer can also be used to <u>gauge your commissions paid to your salespeople</u>. Do you pay them on gross or net revenue? How do you substantiate those numbers (salespeople are all over the numbers that generate their income)? Analysis of these reports will give you (and your sales staff) the figures you need.

#4: Expenses by Vendor   When you know what you a paying to a vendor over a period of time and what you are buying, you have leverage for pricing discounts and payment terms.   A nice discount for paying in ten days can earn you a lot of extra cash.   By examining your vendor costs, you'll have the data you need for these money-saving conversations.

#5: Aging Payables and Receivables   We talked about *payables* and *receivables* in Chapter 11, so this is just a reminder to review these reports on a regular basis. Of course, you want to receive the monies owed to you as soon as possible – and so do your vendors.

> *A budget is telling your money where to go*
> *instead of wondering where it went.*
>
> - Dave Ramsey

#6: <u>Budget v. Actual</u> The only way to know if your company is on track with your goals is to have a Budget and then review your *Budget v. Actual* report. In QB it's easy to set up a Budget. Click on "Company" on the task bar and then open "Planning and Budgeting." From there, you can set up your Budget.

This budget function only applies to your P&L accounts, so loan payments and other obligations on your Liabilities account are NOT included on the budget. Use as many actual figures as you possibly can, such rent, any standing credit card charges (i.e., as Adobe, web hosting, etc.).

After you have set up your budget, you can pull a Budget v. Actual report by going to "Reports" then "Budget." Monthly reviews will give you the data you need to tweak accounts as necessary. For example, you budgeted $75/month for office supplies but you spent $100/month. Why so much more? Look in your supply cabinet and see if there is an excess of supplies. If there's not a surplus , you either:

- Underestimated your office supply needs
- Some office supplies are "walking out the door"

#7: Forecasts   To estimate your company's future growth, and its income and expenses, you should do a *Forecast*, which is much more comprehensive than the Budget and incorporates:

- Amortization and Depreciation
- Balance Sheet
- Breakeven Analysis
- Cash Flow
- Financial Ratios
- Income Statements
- Operating Expenses
- Payroll Costs
- Sales Forecasts
- Startup Expenses

Since Forecasts are more complicated, you would be wise to use a template so you'll have a form into which to post all your data. Score, a part of the Small Business Administration, has a downloadable template at https://www.score.org/resource/financial-projections-template

---

Learn from the past.

See the future.

Make informed decisions.

www.goprophix.com

To be successful,
you have to have your heart in your business
and your business in your heart.

-Thomas Watson, Sr., Chairman and CEO of IBM

CHAPTER 14

Yikes! It's Tax Time

INCOME & PAYROLL TAXES

Taxes don't have to be intimidating if your records are complete and accurate and you have proper documentation for your company's financial activities. There are two major components of taxes: Income Taxes and Payroll Taxes. If you are in retail sales, you may also have Sales Taxes, depending on your state.

Since all companies MUST file an **Income Tax return**, let's review.

Calendar Year: Most companies file their income taxes based on the calendar year[iv] - which begins January 1 and ends December 31. Typically, these types of companies file on the calendar year on these IRS forms:

TYPE of BUSINESS ENTITY	FILES THIS IRS INCOME TAX FORM
Sole Proprietorships	Schedule C of Form 1040
Partnerships	Form 1065 (Form K-1 goes to partners)
Limited Liability Companies	Varies depending on circumstances
S-Corporations	Form 1120-S
Corporations (C-Corps)	Form 1120

Fiscal Year: There are exceptions to filing by the calendar year, and these companies file on their own particular *Fiscal Year*. In other words, the last day of their " business year" is the last day of any month other than December. The IRS frowns on companies that don't file on the calendar year, and you have to get permission from IRS to do so.

An example would be a seasonal business, with income in the spring and expenses in the fall. In this case it might be better to have a fiscal year ending in August so that income and expenses are closely related.[v]

This Workbook is <u>NOT INTENDED</u> to offer tax advice – for that you should see a licensed professional CPA and/or Financial Planner; I am mentioning this here only so that you will be aware of these filing situations.

Generally, when your CPA prepares your taxes, he/she will need these reports from your accounting software for the period being prepared:

1. Income Statement (Profit & Loss)
2. Balance Sheet
3. Trial Balance
4. General Ledger

They may also request the bank statement for the last day of your filing period since there may be transactions on your accounting registers that have not yet cleared your bank.

Companies may have to pay <u>Estimated Taxes</u> depending on their current income and if they expect a tax liability of more than $500 for the year[vi]. Again, this is an issue to discuss with your CPA and/or Financial Planner.

Payroll Taxes   Payroll is one of those functions that is very easy if done correctly and an absolute nightmare if it's not! If you or your bookkeeper are not *comfortable* with this task, do yourself a favor and use a payroll service company. QuickBooks has various levels of payroll assistance and the cost is very reasonable for the services they provide.

One of the hiccups companies incur in handling payroll themselves is failure to pay their payroll tax liabilities in a timely manner and accruing huge penalties and interest. If you use a payroll service, they will automatically take the funds from your checking account to pay these. If you don't want the payroll company to have access to your company's primary checking account, you can set up a separate payroll account and transfer necessary funds to that account when needed. The payroll company will "draw" out the funds for each employee's pay as well as the various liabilities which include:

- Federal tax withholding from employee's pay
- State tax withholding from employee's pay
- FICA – employee portion withheld from employee's pay
- FICA – company matches the employee's withholding
- Medicare – employee portion withheld from employee's pay
- Medicare – company matches the employee's withholding
- Federal unemployment tax paid by your company
- State unemployment tax paid by your company

Here's a summary of the forms used to report these taxes:

FORM	REPORTS THESE TAXES
IRS – 941	Federal withholding
	FICA (both employee w/h and company match)
	Medicare (both employee w/h and company match)
IRS – 940	Federal unemployment
State (form varies by state)	State unemployment
State (form varies by state)	State w/h taxes

When you set up your company and received your **FEIN** (Federal Employer Identification Number) from the federal government you should also have received information about setting up your online *Electronic Funds Transfer Payment System* (**EFTPS**) account. All federal tax payments are made electronically through this system. States have also converted to electronic filings, so check with your state's Department of Revenue for information.

If you are a company doing Union work, you will also be filing *Certified Payroll Reports* and paying all the applicable union dues and other benefits. These, too, can be complicated so be sure your payroll service can provide them. Quickbooks has these reports built in and they take about a minute to prepare if you are using the QB payroll system.

At the end of each calendar year, you will have to provide a Form W-2 to each of your employees – which is also done by your payroll service, if you have one. And your vendors/subcontractors receive a Form 1099. These can also be generated and printed or filed electronically from most accounting software programs.

> *The biggest thrill wasn't in winning on Sunday*
> *but in meeting the payroll on Monday.*
>
> -Art Rooney,
> Founding Owner of the Pittsburgh Steelers

Your employees are vital to the success of your company. One way to take care of them is to be sure you have a good payroll system in place; never get in a situation where an employee has to ask you *When will I get paid?*

CHAPTER 15

Be a Paper Doll

FILING SYSTEM

Most modern companies depend too heavily on computers for file maintenance and don't know how to handle the huge amount of paper created by their operations. As a result, you have so much paper in your office -- on your desk -- and on the floor that you:

> ... can't find that new contract and your client just called with an important question about it!

> ...misplaced the business card the venture capitalist gave you!

> ...lost a schematic chart you need for the meeting that started ten minutes ago!

> ...mistakenly threw away the financials your banker needed yesterday!

> ...started thinking, "Where did all this paper come from?"

According to *INC* magazine, business has more paper to contend with now than ever before. Don't wait until you're in a paper crisis to get your hard copies organized. I understand you're a busy executive and you've got more important things to do than FILE! But paper -- and all those hard copies -- can really cause problems if they aren't where you need them, when you need them.

Want some examples? Here's a few I've encountered:

- A new products company was so emmeshed in handling sales they failed to set up a filing system for thousands of orders. When a customer called with a re-order or complaint, they had no idea where the records were. It was a nightmare and they called me to fix it. Of course, it was impossible to sort 5,000 orders by customer name, so we gave each of them a number and cross-referenced the number to the customer name. In three days, we had a four-drawer filing cabinet full of orders and could retrieve them in seconds.

- A forensic engineer received a critical fax regarding the potential collapse of a new helicopter hangar. He lost the fax. All he knew was that there was a deadline for responding. He took five architects and seven engineers away from their work for two hours to look for the lost fax. I estimated the lost work time for the architects (who billed out at $200/hr) and engineers (who billed at $150/hr) cost the company $4,100.00 – Yikes!! ... all for one piece of paper that was lost.

- The Vice President of Finance for a Fortune 500 had stacks and stacks of files on the floor of his office after a merger. There was a winding path through the papers to get to his desk. No one had any idea what was where. It took me more than three weeks to properly file and cross-reference all the contracts and data in those files and put them in a cabinet where they belonged.

The average executive wastes 15 hours a year just looking for paper. If your billable hour is $200 (and that is low in today's economy) then you are _WASTING $3,000 A YEAR_. And that's your waste alone. Double that figure for each additional employee you have and it soon becomes a significant amount of money. Have I convinced you that a filing system is a good idea?   If so, here are recommend files for a start-up company:

Pendaflex Tab	File Folder Label
Automobile	Auto Repairs
	Purchase/Lease Contract
	Tags & Titles
Banking	Bank Statements
	Deposits / Voided Checks
Credit Cards	Amex * 0001
	Bank of Amer * 0002
Financial	Financial Reports
	Investments
	Owner's Acct.
	Bank Loan
	Line of Credit
Insurance	Auto Insurance
	Liability Insurance
	Workers' Comp. Insurance
	Health Insurance
Legal	Business License
	Corporate Registration
	Lease / Rental Agreement
Taxes	Federal Income Taxes
	State Income Taxes
	Sales Taxes
	Payroll taxes (one file for each form: 940 / 941/ State Labor / State W/H / etc.
	Form 1099 (issued to vendors)
	Form W-2 (issued to employees)
Utilities	Electricity
	Gas
	Internet Connectivity
	Landline Phones
	Cell Phones
Vendors	It you don't have many vendors, use Alphabetical (A-B-C)

When a "vendor's name" is the same as a person's name (ex: Joe Jones Consulting) the correct name in your accounting software and on your file folder is *Joe Jones Consulting,* NOT Jones, Joe Consulting. The only time you should put a "last name" first is on your employee records and customer records (if applicable – see below). All others are legal entities, and should be recorded that way.

This list is by no means everything you'll need or want – but hopefully it will give you an idea of what the basic files are. You'll notice that this list does not include either Customers or Employees. These two groups are usually the largest segments of your filing system and should be kept in a separate file draw or filing cabinet. Employee files should be under lock and key.

For **Customer files**, I like to use customer numbers as the primary data, followed by the customer's last name, such as:

    1001 – JONES, Mary
    1002 – SMITH, John
    1003 – SMITH, Richard

If you have a customer that is another company, you would set it up this way:

    1004 – Joe Jones Consulting
    1005 – Mary Smith Design Services, LLC

Numerical records are very easy to set-up and maintain. Because you file these numerically, it is not only quicker, it also prevents errors that arise due to alphabetical filing. Of course, when you set up your customers in your accounting software, you use this same system.

For your **Employee Files** you will also need one file folder for each employee and, generally, the following forms:

1. Employment Application
2. Employee Information (address, SS#, contacts, etc.)
3. Form W-4 (Withholding Tax Form)
4. Form I-9 (Federal requirement to keep these on file)
5. Reviews or Warning Notices
6. Receipt from Employee of any equipment you provided such as hard hats, lap-tops, cell phones, etc.
7. Timesheets if you use them

Be sure that your **employee files are in a locked filing cabinet**!! They have given you private information on their employee documents and you are responsible for the safe handling and security of this information.

I started out typing and filing and answering the phones for a little nine-person firm.
And that nine-person firm gave me my chance to find my own way.

- Carla Fiorina
CEO of Hewlett-Packard

There are no secrets to

SUCCESS.

It is the result of preparation,

HARD WORK

&

LEARNING FROM FAILURE.

-Colin Powell, Four-Star General, United States Army

CHAPTER 16

Last Word

THIS n' THAT

It is my sincerest wish that you will have a very successful company and that this workbook has helped you to get your accounting on a firm foundation. Here are few *miscellaneous* ideas for you to consider (not in any particular order).

Not all CPA firms are the same: Do yourself a favor and find a CPA firm that is qualified to prepare tax returns and provide financial advice based on your industry. For example: A firm that deals mostly with consultants may be ill equipped to provide expert services to a general contractor. In my experience, the really good firms are ready, willing and able to work with your bookkeeper to set up an accounting system that is applicable to your trade. And this can save you big bucks at tax time if you can provide the proper financial reports to make the CPA's work easier.

The Customer is always right: We all know this is not always true, but when you have a problem with a customer, try to look at the situation from their perspective. Burning bridges is never wise. One poor Google review can kill off dozens of potential clients. Resolve issues in a timely and good-spirited manner.

Timely Customer Refunds: People are always making commitments they can't keep – many times for reasons beyond their control. Stay on their best side by quickly refunding any money you owe them. Down the road, when they can afford to do that project, you'll more than likely be the first one they call.

Good Legal Documents: Before you get your first client and hire your first contractor, you should talk with an attorney who knows your industry and have proper purchase orders and contracts drawn up for your use. **DO NOT** start a job without proper written authorization to be on the client's property.

Documentation beats Discussion every time: I worked for a prominent construction-law attorney who said, "In every case there are five issues: The Facts, The Facts, The Facts, The Facts, and The Facts." And then he would say, "Nothing beats discussion like documentation." Get in the habit of maintaining proper legal records: Contracts, Change Orders, Work Orders, Purchase Orders. *Leave nothing to chance* or *verbal agreement*. You don't want to get into a situation where it's your word against theirs. Documents will prove the issue. I can't stress this enough.

Insurance: Get your insurance in order! There are a variety of insurance coverages you should have depending on the nature of your business. If you are a consultant, get E&O (Errors and Omissions) coverage. If you are a contractor, you'll need General Liability as well as Worker's Compensation insurance, and Umbrella coverage, too. If you are a delivery service, you'll need coverage that exceeds your general Auto policy. Insurance may seem expensive; if you don't have it and there's a claim against you, you'll realize how cheap it really was.

COI's (Certificates of Insurance): This is a standard form used throughout the insurance industry that certifies a company is carrying such and such insurance. When you start a new project or take on a new client, they may ask you for this, so don't be alarmed. Call your insurance agent and give them the name and address of your customer so that the insurance company can issue the COI with your customer named as the "Certificate Holder."

Likewise, if you are a contractor, and hire subcontractors to work on your jobs, you should maintain a binder with the COI from anyone who does any work on any project. This is to protect you and your customer. Be sure that the hired subcontractor has sufficient Worker's Compensation coverage, too. If they come on your job and get hurt, and they don't have insurance, you will be liable and could be stuck with huge medical bills for the injured person. It is not worth the risk!!

Appearance is Everything: What will your banker think when they look at your financial statements and the formatting is all over the place? Sloppy? Is that how you conduct your business? Some accounts might be all *UPPER CASE*, some might be *lower and UPPER Case,* and some might be done properly with UPPER CASE first letter and lower case the remainder of the word. The appearance of your financial statements is a reflection on your company. Here are some examples:

Document / Name	This is sloppy	This looks good
Account Name	assets & Liabilities	Assets & Liabilities
Account Name	OFFICE supplies	Office Supplies
Document	PURCHASE order	Purchase Order
Customer	smith, Jane	Smith, Jane
Vendor	ABc supply	ABC Supply
Date	jan 20 2021	Jan. 20, 2021
Bank	bank of america	Bank of America

Always put your best foot forward and make your company shine with financial records that are a true reflection of you and your business.

The C&C Sandwich: Never open a conversation with a negative comment! If you need to correct a vendor or employee, always start with a compliment. Then you can "sandwich" in the criticism and close the conversation with another compliment. Negative statements and criticisms will always put the other person on the defensive – and the outcome probably won't be what you wanted and will damage your relationship in the long run. Here's an example from my personal experience:

> I was supervising the construction of a very large home and imported Italian stone had been delivered to the jobsite for installation in the grand foyer. Excited to see the work, I stopped by the job and was mortified to see that the tile was installed in a very crooked, out-of-plumb alignment. It looked awful and I knew my clients would have a hissy fit.

> Rather than jumping all over my tile contractor (it took some constraint) I *oohed and aaahed* over the expensive tile. "Wow, that is beautiful tile, isn't it." I was standing in the living room and invited the contractor to look with me. "Isn't that gorgeous?" I enthused. From his new perspective he had the same view I did. He cocked his head to one side, shook it back and forth a few times, and rubbed his chin.

> "Humm," he whispered. "Something doesn't look right." He took out his measuring tape and after several minutes looked up at me from where he knelt in the foyer and said, "I'm so sorry but this is way out of plumb. We're going to have to remove it and start over."

> It was lucky the tile was not completely adhered to the floor and we only lost three pieces. He didn't charge me a penny to re-do the work and I gave him the contract to do the five large bathrooms in the house, and everything was perfect.

We all make mistakes. But given the opportunity to see them our self, and to correct them, makes everyone happier. So, remember this: *Always sandwich criticism with compliments.*

Everyone is Important: There will be times when someone will approach you about using your services and it may be out of you realm. The job may be either too big or too small, or beyond your area of expertise. If you can't do the work for them, please take a few minutes and refer them to someone who can. You never know when they might be a perfect match for you down the road. Here's another story from my archives:

> A young wife was expecting her first child and wanted a nice nursery for the baby. She and her husband didn't have much money, but she had set aside a little money for the project. She called dozens of interior designers and asked for help, but was rebuffed by everyone, "Oh, that's way too small a job." But she persevered, and finally got a small firm who said they would be delighted to do her small project.
>
> Fast forward 15 years. The wife's husband had just sold his company to a software giant and they were building a huge mansion on acreage and she had tons of money to spend. Guess who she called.   "Things have changed since you did that nursery," she told them.

People change and situations change. Being *nice* is timeless.

No one knows everything: Business is constantly evolving and you should be open to new and better ways of doing things so don't limit yourself by thinking you know it all – because no one does! Surround yourself with people who can do what you can't do, or don't know how to do, so that you can concentrate on what you do well. Appreciate everyone who brings their skill to you.

Remember, no company started out as a Fortune 100 or Fortune 500.

- Microsoft started in the garage of college drop-out, Bill Gates.
- Google was started in the dorm room of two college students.
- Coca-Cola was started in drug store by a pharmacist. (His bookkeeper named the drink and penned the script that became the company trademark.)
- AT&T was founded by a teacher of deaf students, Alexander Graham Bell.
- Tom Clancy was an insurance broker; his first book was published when he was 37. He was worth $83 million when he died.
- Amazon was founded by Jeff Bezos to sell books out of his garage.
- Delta Airlines started as Huff Daland Dusters, a crop-dusting company with 18 planes.
- Virgin Airlines was started by Richard Branson who sold $39 one-way tickets to the British Virgin Islands and advertised the sale on a blackboard.

In summary, I offer some advice from some people who know something about business:

Always deliver more than expected.

– Larry Page, co-Founder of Google

Our most unhappy customers are our greatest source of learning.

– Bill Gates, co-Founder of Microsoft

Respect is how you treat everyone, not just those you want to impress.

– Richard Branson, Founder of The Virgin Group

Quality is the best business plan.

– John Lasseter, founder of Pixar

You will either step forward into growth or step back into safety.

– Abraham Maslow, PhD.,
Author of "A Theory of Human Motivation"

GLOSSARY

Accounting Procedures The day-to-day methods of recording financial transactions so that the accounting data will be specified in a consistent manner.

Accounting System The software, procedures, and financial documents used in the recording and maintenance of the company's operations.

Accrual Basis Accounting Recording of transactions when they occur regardless of when cash is paid or received.

Advance Payment Any payment made to a contractor before work has been performed or goods have been delivered.

Automated Clearing House (ACH) Electronic remittance within the banking system.

Balance Sheet A financial report of the assets, liabilities and equity of a company.

Budget Planned income and expenditures during a specific period of time.

CAC Customer acquisition cost.

Cash Currency, checks, postal and express money orders, and banker's drafts on deposit.

Capital Assets Also known as *Fixed* Assets; includes land, buildings, improvements, easements, vehicles, machinery, equipment, and other tangible assets used in the operations of the company; the initial useful life of the capital asset must extend beyond a single reporting period.

Cash Basis Accounting Recognizes transactions when related cash is received or disbursed.

Chart of Accounts A listing of all assets, liability, equity, revenue and expenditure accounts that are used to record financial transactions. Many times, the COA includes numbers.

Depreciation Loss in value of an asset; annual reductions in asset are written off as an expense.

EFTPS   Electronic Funds Transfer Payment System – a US Treasury system for businesses to pay their taxes online.

Electronic Funds Transfer (EFT)   EFT is a system of transferring money from one bank account directly to another without paper money changing hands.

Estimate   A detailed listing of all the materials and labors required to complete a certain project.

Expenditures   Payments for good and services; can be either cash or credit card transactions.

FCC   Federal Communications Commission.

Fixed Assets   See *Capital Assets*.

GAAP   Abbreviation for *Generally Accepted Accounting Principles*, which are the normal procedures and rules for maintaining financial records and creating financial statements.

Income Statement   Also referred to as the *Profit and Loss Statement*; a report of the revenue, COGS, expenses, other income and expenses, and net income for a given period of time.

Profit and Loss Statement   See "Income Statement."

Progress Payments   Partial payments for goods and/or services under contract to be delivered or completed by a certain period of time.

Purchase Order   A document issued by one entity to another to authorize delivery of specified materials and/or labor or service.

Subcontractor   Person or company that provides labor and materials to a job; characterized as a *Vendor* for accounting purposes.

Subsidiary Ledger   A ledger of numerous transactions that roll up into a main or primary account. For example, Accounts Receivable Subsidiary Ledgers are the listings of all customer transactions; each customer has their own *ledger* so that you know the balance they owe. On the Balance Sheet, you only see "Accounts Receivable" which is a total of all customer ledgers.

Vendor   Person or company that sells supplies and materials - does NOT work on a job.

INDEX

OTHER BOOKS BY MARGERY PHELPS

Downline Dynamics – how to build a happy, healthy downline
Contract book for Janiece C. Andrews, MD

Common Sense Medicine – a medical doctor's prescription for health care in America – Ghost writer for Robert A. Nash, MD

Harmony's House – a coloring book (for children)
Illustrations by Tonya Pash and Mike Carney

Halo's Glow (for children)
Illustrations by Aly Hopper

Mighty-Me and the Rainbow Plate (for children)
Illustrations by Julie Weinberger

You don't have to be sick – healthy eating is good medicine
With co-author, Janiece C. Andrews, MD

New Life Naturally, a home guide to harmonious health
With David Allen, Ph.D.

At First Sight – the story behind the MGM Motion Picture
Contract book for Barb and Shirl Jennings, subjects of the movie

Finding Margaret – a case for reincarnation
A narrative non-fiction

Crossing the Bridge from Life to Life
A workbook on reincarnation

Endnotes

[i] https://www.businessnewsdaily.com/2664-accounting-standards.html

[ii] https://www.hubspot.com/

[iii] https://blog.hubspot.com/service/what-does-cac-stand-for

[iv] https://www.nolo.com/legal-encyclopedia/choosing-fiscal-year-your-business.html

[v] https://www.nolo.com/legal-encyclopedia/choosing-fiscal-year-your-business.html

[vi] https://www.irs.gov/businesses/small-businesses-self-employed/estimated-taxes

www.ingramcontent.com/pod-product-compliance
Lightning Source LLC
Chambersburg PA
CBHW051415200326
41520CB00023B/7242

9780999462218